WORCESTERSHIRE

BROMYARD DOWNS

A44

Bromyard

River Frome

A4103

Malvern

dlow

nster

...nd

...at this lovely

...the facilities, attractions and
accommodation please vist:

www.visitherefordshire.co.uk

Tel: 01432 260621
Fax: 01432 363031

HEREFORDSHIRE

A Little Souvenir

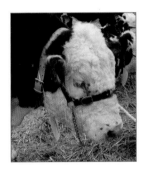

CHRIS ANDREWS PUBLICATIONS

HEREFORDSHIRE

Marden Church from Sutton Walls

Herefordshire

Even compared with its English neighbours Gloucestershire, Shropshire and Worcestershire, Herefordshire is exceptional in having kept so much of its natural beauty. Factories, retail parks and spreading suburbs are less in evidence than elsewhere. The motorway network hardly touches it (a short stretch of the M50 runs from the Gloucestershire border to Ross-on-Wye).

Tourism has not much affected its small towns and villages. The landscape is green and pleasant: gentle wooded hills, meadows and streams offer a perfect image of a rural England that is fast disappearing elsewhere. With under sixty thousand inhabitants its chief city, Hereford, has the atmosphere of a country town.

Herefordshire has well defined borders: in the east the Bromyard Downs and the western slopes of the Malverns; in the south the Forest of Dean; to the north lie the Shropshire Hills and to the west the mountains of Wales. It is rich in streams and

The Cathedral of Our Lady and Saint Ethelbert in Hereford has a chained library containing the Mappa Mundi, a Medieval map of the world

rivers. The Teme crosses a small part of the north of the county, but the main rivers in its northern half are the Arrow, Frome and Lugg. All flow southwards and, directly or indirectly, into the Wye, which, rising in Wales, twists and turns eastward to Hereford, and then, still twisting and turning flows southwards towards the Severn. It was the Wye Valley that inspired the first British tourist guide, written by William Gilpin in

1782. It also provided inspiration for Pope, Coleridge, Wordsworth and the painter J M W Turner.

The outstanding buildings are usually in sandstone or are timber-framed. The cathedral, Goodrich Castle and Berrington Hall are splendid examples of sandstone. The black and white villages of Eardisland, Pembridge and

6 View from Symonds Yat rock

Weobley, among many others, are picturesque without being self-consciously quaint. For a county with a small population, there is an astonishing variety of churches: from grand medieval buildings such as the cathedral and Dore Abbey to the Rococo Gothic of Shobdon, the nineteenth-century Italian Romanesque of Hoarwithy and the twentieth-century Arts and Crafts Gothic at Brockhampton-by-Ross. All these are equalled by the two almost perfectly preserved Norman village churches at Kilpeck and Moccas.

Equally astonishing is the number of castles, country houses and gardens encompassing all periods from the Middle

Old House Museum and St Peter's, Hereford   7

Herefordshire from the western slopes of the Malverns

Ages onwards. The National Trust and English Heritage are both well represented in the county. Cymmau Farmhouse, Croft Castle, Berrington Hall, Lower Brockhampton Manor and the Weir Gardens all belong to the Trust, while the castles at Goodrich, Longtown and Wigmore are in the care of English Heritage, as are Arthur's Stone, a Neolithic tomb, and Rotherwas Chapel. Burton Court, Eastnor Castle, Hampton Court Gardens, Hellen's, and Hergest Croft Gardens are in private ownership but open to the public.

Herefordshire has strong musical links with its neighbours. Its cathedral shares the annual Three Choirs Festival – the

10 Hereford: Old House Museum and All Saints' Church

oldest in Europe – with its sister cathedrals of Gloucester and Worcester. Edward Elgar, born just over the border in Worcestershire, lived in Hereford between 1904 and 1911, a period during which he composed, among many great works, his two symphonies and his violin concerto.

However, for all its links with music and literature – Ledbury was home to the poets William Langland, Elizabeth Barrett-Browning and John Masefield while Thomas Traherne, born in Hereford, was rector at Credenhill – Herefordshire is above all associated with agriculture. More than anything else cider apples, hops and Hereford cattle evoke the county.

An often overlooked county, Herefordshire has much of which to be proud, in terms of unspoilt landscapes, great houses and gardens, country parks and animal sanctuaries, cultural activities and outdoor pursuits from walking, cycling and horse-riding to more adventurous activities such as water sport and gliding.

Hereford: carving over the entrance to the Market Hall   11

12 Hereford Cathedral and the River Wye. Much repaired and reinforced, the bridge
dates from 1490

The Cathedral Close: Dr Elgar and 'Mr Phoebus'. During the Elgars' stay in Hereford (1904 - 1911) Edward's chief relaxation was cycling: rides of 50 miles were not uncommon. He called his first bicycle 'Mr Phoebus'.

Eaton Bishop: according to Pevsner this church has the finest decorated stained glass in the county. He praises its "sophisticated, highly emotional draughtsmanship".

Madley: the east end of the Church of The Nativity of the Virgin.   15

16 Tyberton

18 The Weir Gardens lie on a bend of the River Wye

Hergest Ridge runs westwards from Kington to Gladestrey in Wales. Walkers, cyclists and horse riders all make use of its grassy summit. Mike Oldfield named an album after the area   19

20 Ponies on Hergest Ridge

22 Herefordshire has some of the most picturesque black and white villages in England. Many good examples are found between Kington and Leominster: this is Dilwyn

Eardisland in autumn   23

From Hergest Ridge looking northwards towards Shropshire

26 Bowls at Eardisland

River Arrow at Eardisland 27

28   Pembridge: typical black and white buildings

Pembridge: some unpainted timber-framed buildings   29

30 **Weobley Church from the north**

Defying trends in rural life, Weobley is a thriving village. It has a filling station, pubs, cafes and a wide range of shops, including one that sells new and second-hand books

32   Shobdon Church, a perfect example of Rococo Gothic

34   The gardens at Berrington Hall

Wigmore Church from the castle   35

38   Leominster: the Old Butter Market (1634)

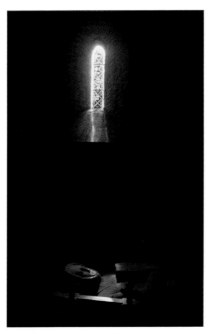

Edwyn Ralph Church   39

From Merbach Hill looking westwards towards Wales

42   Edvin Loach in spring

Dawn on the Bromyard Downs   43

44   Lower Brockhampton

The Herefordshire Beacon from Colwall   45

46   Herefordshire from the Worcestershire side of the Malverns

Looking towards the Malverns from Ledbury   47

48   Ledbury: Church Lane leads logically to the Church of St Michael, one of the grandest parish churches in Herefordshire

Ledbury is known for its outstanding timber-framed buildings   49

50 The Norman church of Kilpeck has an astonishing range of carvings which reveal Celtic, Anglo-Saxon and Viking influences

Much Marcle: the tomb of Blanche Mortimer who died in 1347. Its timeless serenity contrasts with the carvings at Kilpeck

52 Prize Herefords at Kington Show

Cider Press, Weston's Cider, Much Marcle   53

54   Hoarwithy, St Catherine: The church was rebuilt in the second half of the 19th century in the Italian Romanesque style.

Brockhampton, All Saints is as unexpected as Hoarwithy. It was built in 1901-2 in the Arts and Crafts tradition

Kerne Bridge near Goodrich

58   Ross on Wye

Ross on Wye: the church of St Mary overlooks the river   59

60   Ross: Wilton Bridge

The "Man of Ross" is celebrated in a poem by Coleridge. The sculpture, by Walenty Pytel, has stood on the bank of the Wye since the late 1990's

62   Goodrich Castle. Begun after the Norman Conquest and extended during the following centuries, it was slighted during the Civil War. However it is more than a romantic ruin, having some well-preserved medieval interiors and modern stained glass

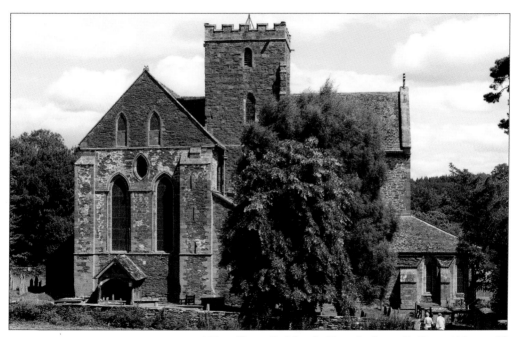

Abbey Dore: St Mary's Church, formally Dore Abbey   63

First published 2008 by Chris Andrews Publications Ltd

15 Curtis Yard North Hinksey Lane Oxford OX2 0LX

Telephone: +44(0)1865 723404 **www.cap-ox.co.uk**

Photos: Philip Ruler Text: Philip Ruler Map: Mike Brain Graphic Design Ltd © Chris Andrews Publications Ltd

ISBN 978-1-905385-70-6

Thanks to Andrea Hammersley, Lynda and Philip Lynne and David Snoswell. Penguin for permission to qoute from
Herefordshire by Nikolaus Pevsner, Penguin Books Ltd 1968. © Nikolaus Pevsner 1968.

Front Cover: Symonds Yat   Title page: Hereford Bull   This page:Arthur's Stone, Dormston   Back cover: Ledbury

Herefordshire

This endpaper shows the south of the area pictured in this book. The endpaper at the front of the book shows the northern area covered.